That's Life - Deal With It

A Guide

Dr. Gil Anderson

authorHOUSE®

AuthorHouse™
1663 Liberty Drive, Suite 200
Bloomington, IN 47403
www.authorhouse.com
Phone: 1-800-839-8640

First published by AuthorHouse 6/11/2009

ISBN: 978-1-4389-5066-2 (sc)

Library of Congress Control Number: 2009901421

Printed in the United States of America
Bloomington, Indiana

This book is printed on acid-free paper.

About the Author

Dr. Gilbert W. Anderson is a board-certified clinical psychologist with years of public and private practice experience. He is also a graduate of a theological seminary, which enables him to combine theology and psychology in his work. Dr. Anderson brings years of experience as a psychologist, pastor, teacher, counselor, and administrator in mental health services and higher education. He consults with educational institutions, religious organizations, industry, and hospitals and has a unique insight into human needs and behaviors. He is well-known as a knowledgeable and entertaining seminar presenter and speaker. He continues to council and lecture in his home on the Eastern shore of the Chesapeake Bay.

Preface

"I'm not prepared for this!"

How many times have you encountered a transition, trauma, or major life event and felt completely helpless – or worse, hopeless? You've heard the old saying, "life is a journey" but have you ever really thought about what those words actually mean?

The road of life is different for each human being. For some it has a smooth, predictable course while others know constant struggle and sacrifice. Sometimes an easy road can take a wicked turn. Out of the blue some unexpected and life-changing event occurs – a divorce, a death, a tragic illness or accident – and the path is forever altered. When this happens, one of the most common thoughts is: "I'm not prepared for this!"

For decades social scientists have studied the stages of human development in an attempt to understand when and why we learn. It is now generally accepted that prenatal development prepares individuals to cope with the physical environment. Following birth, the human body learns to adapt to light and changes in temperature and sound. An awareness of smell is acquired. As children grow they learn to eat, walk, talk, and become toilet trained. They learn to socialize with the immediate family, and, later, with less familiar people. This learning lasts far beyond traditional learning years. Well past high school people are expanding their socialization skills while learning to be emotionally and financially independent.

While most people eventually learn to be socially adept and economically responsible, our training rarely prepares us for the series of difficult and life-changing events we all eventually will face.

That's Life – Deal With It is intended to make you more aware of the personal challenges that are a part of everyday living and to provide suggestions for managing them so you can *Deal With It!*

Chapters In Brief

It would be foolish to claim to address *all* of life's challenges, but the ten presented in *That's Life – Deal With It* arose out of a lifetime of counseling people. These were the challenges most often presented in counseling sessions. The following is a summary of these.

Chapter 1   1

The Strongest Human Drive evolved due to the large numbers of clients who felt totally helpless and were unable to identify their true needs. This chapter examines the strongest human drive.

Chapter 2   9

Establishing Life Priorities was a problem frequently presented by people who had no clear value system. They did not know how to decide what was really important to them.

Managing Personal Relationships was a recurrent theme in therapy. Relating positively with other people, selecting and living happily with a mate are clearly challenging, since national statistics indicate that about half of all marriages in the United States end in divorce.

Sexual Adjustments are serious concerns for most people. They often do not understand the changes encountered as sexual relationships progress and they frequently stumble through them.

Children for a Lifetime addresses parenthood, which is a common theme in therapy for individuals and couples. Maintaining a marriage with children can be perplexing.

His and Her Mid-Life Transitions presents the myriad of adjustments people experience in their middle years. The "empty nest" and living as husband and wife again after raising children is addressed.

Aging Parents is an issue for an increasingly significant percentage of our population. Deciding what to do with parents who need help is a concern, as is coping with guilt.

Chapter 1

The Strongest Human Drive

What really drives the human mind and body is not sex, not even the will to live, but the need for control. First and foremost, we all want to survive. Once we are comfortable and content in mind and body, our thoughts can turn toward human pleasures.

Take a moment and think back to a time when you might have been in a dangerous or even life-threatening situation. What was foremost in your mind at the time? It was probably not sex, but survival. How you were going to avoid danger, prevent an accident, stop the bleeding, administer CPR, or help an injured child or friend – this is what you were focused on. Name the situation and try to recall what your strongest instinct was for those precious moments. If you still answered sex, put down this book and call a counselor or the Jerry Springer Show. You need some help. For those of you who did not answer sex, please read on. There's hope for you.

The will to live is an extremely strong drive. Even so, there are times and situations when individuals come to the conclusion that all hope is lost – and they are willing to give up their lives. When someone has been self-sufficient and functional his entire life, it is difficult to accept that he is no longer so. It feels frustrating and embarrassing to be forced suddenly to be dependent and unable to take basic care of one's self. Some people feel that they would be better off dead, and they gradually become ready to die rather than go through the pain, the embarrassment of diaper pads, of being bathed, and of being pushed around in a wheelchair. Suicide is a desperate final attempt to take control.

Loss of Control

During my years as a psychological consultant to hospitals and nursing homes, I have encountered many people who were so discouraged that they thought they would rather die than struggle with conditions which took away their independence and control. Often I have visited people who were ill or elderly in health care facilities who were very depressed over "no longer being the person I have always been." They usually greeted me by saying, "I'm no longer myself; get out and let me die." What they were expressing were feelings that they no longer had enough control over their lives to let them function as they had throughout their adult lives. They were depressed about this dramatic change in their circumstances.

On one occasion I was requested to visit and counsel a fifty-five-year-old female who had experienced a stroke. I was told that she needed treatment for depression. I entered her room, introduced myself, and explained why I was visiting her. She responded by pointing to the door, indicating by motion that she wanted me to leave. I quickly observed that the stroke had affected her left side and her speech.

I said that probably the stroke had made her feel helpless, frightened, and depressed, and that, if she would permit me to stay, I might be able to help her. She began to weep and motioned for me to stay.

A stroke is clearly frightening and frustrating at any age, and possibly more so for a younger person. This lady was depressed over her loss of control. During several months of counseling and speech and physical therapy, she regained enough ability to speak and walk such that her attitude became much more positive. What changed? She felt that she had some control in her life again.

Another case which illustrates how loss of control affects people is about a man in his 70s who was diabetic. I was asked to help him cope emotionally with the amputation of two toes on his right foot. With counseling, he was able to face that loss. Then, to his dismay, he learned that eventually he would lose more toes, his foot, and then his lower leg. All of these surgeries took place over several months.

Counseling and physical therapy helped, but even though he lived, he never overcame his depression resulting from the loss of control. He felt that he would never again be the person he had always been.

One elderly woman I visited regularly shared three statements regarding the loss of control:
"Aging is for the brave."
"It's hell to get old."
"I wish I could die."

The Process

The series of emotional stages of loss of control are as follows:

1. Control
2. Helplessness
3. Fear
4. Anger
5. Anxiety
6. Depression
7. Death

Let's study the stages.

1. Control

    Control is our strongest drive. Have you ever watched a turtle on its back? It stretches every part of its body trying to regain control. Humans behave much the same way. They try so hard that they become frantic and anxious.

2. Helplessness

    People are not usually aware of it, but although the feeling of helplessness is terribly frightening, often their reaction to it is anger.

3.   Fear

Have you ever been so angry that it was eating you up inside? It was because you were extremely frightened to have lost control, or your control was being threatened.

4.   Anger

The basis of most anger is a fear of a loss of control over a valued situation such as a job, a marriage, the management of a child, failing health, etc. Many people are not usually aware of the fear because they immediately explode in anger. It is the fight or flight response.

5.   Anxiety

Like the turtle, people will frantically try every technique that comes to mind in order to regain control. They often find themselves in a tornado of fear and anger which leads to anxiety. Anxiety has been proven to exhaust us. It has also been found to contribute to detrimental physical responses such as headaches, high blood pressure, digestive problems, heart disease, hypoglycemia, and diabetes.

6.   Depression

Most people who are extremely anxious become aware that the anxiety is causing them harm. What often follows is a depressive state. Frequently they say, "Well, at least I am no longer anxious." This conclusion is wrong. Depression is a common response to the inability to regain control. It can simply be a subliminal form of anxiety.

It should be noted that some people suffer from depression because of chemical imbalance.

One day I was called to a rehabilitation hospital on a consult regarding a problem patient. Nursing staff described the patient's behavior as "grumpy old man." The gentleman, "Fred," began each day by being belligerent and uncooperative with the nursing staff. Fred was irritable, demanding and depressed in the morning, and the nurses dreaded encountering him at that time of day. They requested that Fred be prescribed an antidepressant so his mornings would be better.

I inquired about Fred's waking glucose level, based on my knowledge that high or low glucose levels can affect mood. That test had never been ordered.

The lab report on Fred's waking sugar levels, measured in milligrams per deciliter of blood, over three days was consistently low, ranging from the upper 40s to lower 60s. The normal range is 90 – 110. Based on the report, I suggested that the nursing staff greet Fred with a glass of orange juice each morning as he was waking up. The juice worked beautifully. Fred was much more positive in the morning now, no antidepressant required. Just orange juice.

Some people experience unfounded depression; they are depressed without any clear cause. However, the majority of depression is a result of fear of loss of control of some life element, such as employment, divorce, health, etc.

7.   Death

If patients remain depressed long enough, with no counseling or any hope of regaining control, their health problems can increase in number and significance. In some instances this can lead to serious illness and even death.

So, what actions can people take to "deal with it?" The following chapters address a number of life situations during which it is common to lose control, and suggestions about how to "deal" with each one. The final chapter further discusses the progression of loss of control, and includes coping attitudes which offer hope to anyone who is struggling with feelings of lost control.

Chapter 2
Establishing Life Priorities

What do you want your life to be like? Children frequently say they want to be a fireman, policeman, or astronaut when they grow up. During my years as a college dean I often watched students struggle to decide on an academic major. The registrar at the University of Arizona in Tucson recently observed that during a four year tenure, students often have changed their minds at least three times before finally settling on one late in their junior year or in their senior year.

Establishing life values is seldom a concern for recent high school and college graduates. They are usually searching for employment, moving to a new location, or considering marriage. A long-lasting value system usually comes later in life, if at all.

In private practice many clients came to me seeking help regarding problems which might never have developed if they had been following a life value system. Their primary goal was to become employed at either of the two large factories in the area with little thought or planning about much else.

A frequent statement by many local high school students and people in low paying jobs was, "I'm going to get on at one of the plants." Even those who had spent years in lower level jobs continued to dream about "getting on at" one of the plants.

It is not often that people consciously and seriously consider life goals and priorities in their youth or indeed at any time in their lives. Most people operate on ideals such as obtaining more money, raising their children, buying a house, paying off their mortgage. They rarely systematically develop a list of goals for life.

Amy

When I was a community college counselor, "Amy" came to my office one day. Amy was an attractive young lady, about eighteen, and a better-than-average student. She had come to tell me that she was strongly considering dropping out of college. When I asked her why, she said that she had a horse. She could not afford to pay her tuition, fees, and school expenses and still maintain her horse. So she felt the best action was to quit school.

Intrigued by Amy's logic, I asked her to think about all the various elements in her life. It was apparent that her thoughts were focused on her horse rather than herself. But to obtain a clearer picture of her thinking I asked her to write down five priorities she felt she could not live without. Her assignment for our next session was to identify these and list them in order of importance.

Amy returned the next week and shared her list with me. It was a bit surprising.

Amy's List
1. My horse
2. My dog
3. My parents
4. My education
5. Myself

At that moment I knew that Amy's biggest obstacle was not her horse or even her school finances, but the lack of attention to priorities for her life.

We discussed her values and their sustainability over the next ten years. Ten years seems to be about as long as most priorities remain constant. In my experience, values change and require review and revision approximately every decade – or more often.

Her horse was already fifteen years old. It might live another ten years, but Amy agreed that even that was questionable. In fact, the horse would not likely be in good health if it lived longer.

Her dog was already eight years old and she agreed that he would not likely live another ten years.

She said her parents were already old and would probably not survive another ten years. I learned later that her parents were actually in their fifties, yet she was certain they would not live ten more years. I found her views on age and aging most entertaining.

Fourth on Amy's list was her education. She was willing to withdraw from college in order to keep her horse. Such a decision would have meant the loss or postponement of any further education.

She put herself last. She was totally unclear about her future and what her identity might be in ten years.

After several more counseling sessions, Amy came to realize that her current priorities were untenable over ten years. She became convinced that she needed a more durable set of values. During several more sessions, she developed n new list of priorities for her life.

Amy's New List

God

1. Self

2. Education

3. Career

4. Love – G&R

5. Religious foundation

Her first priority was now herself. She felt some guilt over this. It made her feel selfish and she quoted Jesus, saying, "deny yourself and follow me." I reminded her that even Jesus, who had the power to work miracles, had to maintain himself. Jesus was often surrounded by a large group of people seeking his healing touch. On more than one occasion, he left the crowd to step into a small boat and go off in solitude to eat, sleep, and pray. It only made sense that he withdraw and refresh himself in order to be strong and effective the next day.

Amy eventually realized that she owed it to those she loved to maintain herself so she could perform at her best the next day. She overcame her feelings of guilt about putting herself first. She understood that maintaining herself insured that her life in general would be more effective. She comprehended the difference between blatant selfishness and the practical attitude of keeping herself strong and productive.

Her second value, education, was vital to prepare her to earn a living and seek a better life. She realized that now was the best time to pursue her education.

Selecting a career was important in order for her to have definitive direction. She decided to become a physical education teacher.

In discussing her next priority: Love – G&R, she explained that love was vital, but is incomplete without both Giving and Receiving. She said she thought that complete love includes both.

A religious foundation was Amy's final value selection. She was sure that this item would give full meaning to her life, and that the other four values would be incomplete without having a relationship to a "higher power." She also placed God as an umbrella over the entire list.

The Test

We then applied the ten year test to her new value list. If she put herself first in a practical way, she should survive another ten years. In pursuing education, she would retain all its benefits during those ten years and longer.

Her career as a physical education teacher would also be sustainable since physical education is a basic course offered in most American schools.

As far as her next value, Love, she was already in a loving relationship with a fellow student, and she felt certain that the relationship would continue another ten years and longer.

Her relationship with God, she said, would survive another ten years, and for eternity.

She felt that her new value and priority system prepared her much better for the next ten years than had her initial one. She remained in college and recognized that she should review and adjust her value list as she progressed to marriage, parenthood, midlife, and retirement.

If people would set up a value system early on, they could potentially avoid some major obstacles. An example can be found in retirement planning. In consulting with a large manufacturing plant, I was asked to talk with employees who were one year away from their thirty-year retirement dates. In one meeting, there were about 150 near-retirees in attendance. I asked who had a savings plan. Only three in the whole group had any plan beyond pension and Social Security. They were proud to have their houses paid off, but had no savings. I encouraged the company to initiate the retirement sessions ten years before retirement, so that at least the workers would have that long to do some financial planning and enjoy retirement more comfortably.

The act of developing a value and priority system looks simple, but it is more challenging than it appears. This exercise can be vital to a marriage or any other significant relationship. It is certain that individuals will have their own values, systematic or not. Husbands and wives are often surprised to find how their values differ. But getting to know the priorities of a person with whom we share a life is vital to a healthy relationship. Sharing priorities with each other improves communication. During my years of counseling people, I learned that a review of the priorities between life partners about every six months resulted in vastly improved communication. An open dialogue helps when making mutual decisions about such things as job changes, new or second homes, retirement plans, and so on.

Chapter 3
Managing Personal Relationships

Communication

We talk a lot about relationships. But we don't normally talk about how to develop and maintain them. Even college level psychology courses rarely include the subject of choosing a mate and maintaining that relationship under positive and negative conditions. Unfortunately, much of what we learn about relationships is derived through trial and error over time, without ever considering some basic dynamics.

Some say, "do others before they do you." Yet considering others is more effective over time. Sincere communication is most effective as we talk to each other, get to know the other person's likes and dislikes, interests, goals, and fears. Without regular daily communication and sharing of feelings, frustration and resentment can build up, and the chances of building a positive relationship diminish. (The same can be said for prayer to God. Regular communication is the only way to have a positive relationship with God.) Sharing feelings requires effort and practice. As we practice, we improve our awareness of our own feelings and our ability to verbalize them. Healing in psychotherapy most often takes place as people become aware of their feelings and are able to express them. The process of searching for the words to describe their feelings and then giving voice to them gives people relief because they feel that they have some control over their concerns. Remember, control is the strongest human drive. When we feel that we have some control in our everyday lives, we feel more confident, and stress and worry are reduced.

Genetics and Environment

The philosopher John Locke once said that when we are born our personalities are undeveloped. He described personality as a blank slate ready for a lifetime of "writing," the product of environment and experience. The early Christian church followed Locke's philosophy. The church decided that the early years of a child are the most important time for writing upon his personality chalkboard. Thus early church training, catechism, confirmation, and church schooling became an integral part of living.

Since Locke, theories of human behavior have come to include genetic as well as environmental influences as sources of the "writing" on a personality. It is clear that all human beings become the people they are because of genetic and environmental influences. Therefore it is vital for people who are developing and maintaining relationships to be aware of the writing on their own chalkboards. Part of this process of awareness is for people to learn how to read and interpret what is there.

Introspection

You cannot read your personality unless you are able to be introspective. Think about how many people you know who are able to look at their identities realistically and accurately perceive and express what they see. It is impossible, for instance, for some people to apologize to someone they have offended because they either refuse or are unable to be introspective without biased attitudes. When faced with a situation that clearly requires an apology, they become nervous or angry.

Introspection requires willingness – and practice. People can learn to accurately read their own personalities when they sincerely want to. Then they can work on sharing their feelings by practicing verbalizing them with someone they trust or at least to themselves in a mirror.

Mate Selection

Introspection is vital to relationships, and no more so than in the initial selection of a mate. There are subtle influences of which we are often unaware which may cause us to be drawn to or to refrain from certain people.

Choosing a life mate is a challenge, and we have little if any training in that area. Consider the divorce rate in the United States at over 50% according to federal statistics.

Over the years, as I have observed couples, I have noticed that many older couples tend to look like brother and sister. Some people conclude that couples look alike because they have lived together for so many years.

Recently in church I noticed an elderly couple. They each sat in the same position as the other, held their mouths the same way, and facially resembled each other. They each also had the same rather unhappy facial expression. Without interviewing them, I can't know why they looked so unhappy. But whatever the reason, they looked alike.

For over twenty years I have studied the newspaper photos of engagement and wedding announcements. I have concluded that over 80% look like they could be brother and sister.

One of the subtle influences at work regarding mate selection is that many people are attracted to people who physically resemble a person in their family who played a significant role — positive or negative – in their life.

It has been postulated that men are attracted to women who are like their mothers, and women are attracted to men who remind them of their fathers. Frequently this is accurate, but not always. I have observed that the attraction can be toward one who is similar to the parent who was *dominant* during the developmental years, father or mother for either men or women.

Alcoholism

Recovering alcoholics have observed that a child raised in a home with an alcoholic parent, father or mother, is extremely likely to marry an alcoholic. Even if neither is a practicing alcoholic, one is predictably likely to become one or to develop another addiction at some point.

Usually alcoholics and criticism go together. Chemical addiction is one part of alcoholism. Another factor is perfectionism. My observation is that most if not all alcoholics are also extremely critical and perfectionist. Alcoholics drink partly because it helps them tolerate imperfection. It is very difficult if not impossible to please an alcoholic. So criticism is a given in the life of a child who grows up in a home with an alcoholic. That child may or may not become an alcoholic, but he is likely to be a critical person himself, and to be attracted to people who are critical. He has never felt he has done anything right and he connects with people who perpetuate his feelings of failure. An adult child of an alcoholic may find people who are not addictive or critical to be boring or unattractive. If the goal is a stable and fulfilling life with a partner, however, learning to accept that less-exciting is really just peaceful is a huge step towards happiness and satisfaction.

Denial of Self

Falling in love overnight can result in a long and happy relationship, but mate selection usually requires significant time for the couple to become more thoroughly acquainted. There is still always a guarantee that there will be adjustments and compromises no matter how well the couple knows each other.

Young people usually are more willing to compromise and adjust to please their mates. Compromise is predictable. The young frequently think that over time they can change or learn to tolerate the negative habits and characteristics of their mates. During that time many compromises are endured and denial of self continues – and, really, no one can change another person without their consent. Denial of self becomes more and more difficult as time passes and resentment builds.

Most people eventually arrive at an age when they feel that life is passing too quickly. It is at that stage when people decide that they are no longer going to compromise. This is the time when it is common for a marriage to encounter a crisis because one person has changed and doesn't want to "take it anymore."

Why tolerate compromises for years, then object to them when many of them can be identified and addressed during the dating period? Remember: keep communicating.

Your value system (see Chapter 2) provides a standard by which to evaluate situations where compromises arise. If you compromise on the first date and it causes you discomfort, make note of it. Discomfort can mean feelings of anger, frustration, a need to retreat, or even physical pain. (As to the latter, the location of the pain is significant. That often is the place in your body where a medical problem is likely to develop later.) If you compromise again on the second date and your reaction is negative, take note again. If by the third date your compromises continue and you feel the same discomfort or pain, it is a signal to initiate a serious discussion with your new friend and express your concerns. After counseling people for nearly forty years, I have concluded that if compromises and pain continue through the dating period, you will benefit by running for your life and beginning a search for a new best friend.

Assertion

It is almost inevitable that one reaches a stage when the "doormat" role has become deeply resented. Bitter resentment or potential divorce is not the way most of us want to approach later years with a spouse.

Compromise that hurts can often be remedied by being assertive. Usually the compromising person is passive and willing to defer. Painful compromises can go on for twenty, thirty, forty years and end in a blow-up. This hostility turns to violence, unproductive and self-defeating decisions, or physical illness.

Rather than exploding with temper tantrums, assertion can be the answer. It is rare that one must be extremely assertive or aggressive early in a relationship. As the passive person practices his ability to be gradually more assertive in a relationship, his ability to stand up for himself improves. The search for effective words, which are assertive but spoken in a way meant not to offend, is a skill which will save the otherwise passive person much grief. Learning to be mildly assertive, then more assertive, and finally highly assertive takes time and practice. The aggressive response is appropriate only when various levels of assertion have failed to communicate.

I was born and raised in Indiana. In my hometown there was enough room for everyone. There were very few lines and little intense competition except in basketball. At age twenty-three I moved to Philadelphia to attend a Presbyterian seminary. My early days there were miserable. My fellow students were mostly East Coast natives who were very competitive, even when there seemed to be no need for it.

I was shocked one day as I was backing my car into a parallel parking space when a driver behind me pulled forward into the space blocking me from it. I moved forward and he took the space. Please be assured that I never allowed that to happen to me again.

Another time I was in a subway car, where there was an elderly lady standing next to me. A seat became available near us, and I motioned for her to take it. Before she could move toward it, another person behind us shoved us both out of the way and dove into the seat.

Once I had a grocery cart partly loaded. I stepped away from it to reach for an item, and returned to find a lady taking items out of my cart. When I confronted her, she said some of what she wanted was no longer on the shelf so she was taking them from my cart.

Eastern Seaboard natives have been characterized as "pushy." I became very "pushy" living there. It took about a year for me to realize that the culture in Philadelphia was not aggressive, but in fact much more assertive than I had experienced in the Midwest. I spent another nine years in Philadelphia and am grateful for the assertion that I learned there.

Positive relationships require developing a personal value system, learning to identify and verbalize feelings, practicing assertion, and, above all, communicating.

Chapter 4
Sexual Adjustments

Of course there is a chapter on sex. Some say, "Sex, sex, sex – is that all anyone talks about?" There are other topics, but sex is a primary subject for most people. It is logical that this topic should be included in a chapter on relationships. However, the human sex drive affects nearly everyone throughout the stages of life, single, living together, or married. Thus, the separate chapter.

Oh, the dread parents can feel when they realize that the time has come for them to have a talk with their child about sexual matters. Some go into more detail, others less. The children dread the discussion too and hope that it isn't detailed or personal. Generally all parties are uncomfortable during the conversation and are relieved when it is over. Often children learn more from their peers than they do from their parents regarding the basics of sex. Sex education at home and in schools continues to evolve.

Morality

Moral attitudes and implications are just as important as avoiding sexually transmitted diseases and pregnancy.

Most religious groups teach that it is immoral to have sex before marriage. Some people describe sex as "dirty" and "nasty." Their children frequently enter marriage with that attitude. Even those who have experienced and enjoyed sex before marriage feel that it is wrong or dirty, and feel guilty about it. It can take sincere effort over several years of marriage for many of these grown children to overcome the "dirty" attitude toward sex. The "dirty" attitude usually does not go away on the honeymoon, nor do the feelings of guilt.

I once was acquainted with a young single Christian woman who was dating a Christian man. One day the woman told me that she was pregnant by her boyfriend. She was depressed, frightened, and embarrassed. I asked her if they had used any protection. She responded with surprise and irritation and said, "Oh, that would be planned sin! We weren't planning to sin and have sex; it just happened."

People who hold little if any negative moral attitudes toward pre-marital sex have concerns about avoiding unwanted pregnancies and diseases, and they usually want to finish their education before they marry.

Whatever the couple's attitude toward sex upon entering marriage, it takes time to become comfortable with it, assuming there was no premarital sex. Just getting to know each other's sexual needs and learning to respond takes time, patience, and effort.

Early in the marriage sexual activities are more spontaneous. Many couples look back at their early days and laugh about how often and in what "crazy" places they had sex. They look back because as time passes, work and family schedules begin to inhibit spontaneous sex. Those who were sexually active before marriage will need to be creative in order to avoid boredom.

Pregnancy

The decision to try for a baby often leads to more sexual adjustments. Some couples become pregnant before they are ready while others achieve pregnancy within a few months of the decision.

A significant number of couples have frustrating difficulties beginning a family. Continuing to try and fail is discouraging and inconvenient. Lots of preparation and planning go into each attempt. Men may have to go through the process of sperm count, which can be embarrassing and inconvenient. If the count is low, vitamins and medications are required along with periods of abstinence during which the count increases. Sometimes those sperm need to be saved up for a valiant try. They are probably lifting weights and swimming laps.

Following the ovulation cycle of the woman can also be inconvenient. All of this scheduling and planning severely interrupts spontaneous lovemaking. One couple told me about their struggle which included the husband dutifully taking his vitamins and refraining from any sexual activity. The wife would track her ovulation cycle, checking her temperature. On the day of ovulation, she would call her husband at work and let him know that he needed to come home immediately to try again.

Frequently he would leave work, rush home, and perform. Not much romance on those occasions. Saving sperm, checking temperature, and bracing to perform when all elements are in position to possibly succeed in a pregnancy is trying, wearing, and unromantic. In some cases this goes on for years. Currently there are new procedures and medications being developed to help achieve pregnancy more easily.

Sex During Pregnancy

A successful pregnancy is a happy moment. Then along come new concerns, like, Can we have intercourse? If yes, how often, how energetic, how many months into the pregnancy? Couples vary in this area, some having regular intercourse, others, never. One couple told me they had sex one hour before the wife went to the hospital for delivery.

The Newborn

Next comes the new baby, if all goes well with the pregnancy. There goes most romantic sex again, at least for a while. Mother needs to heal, the baby is adjusting to life outside the womb, and both parents are tired and need sleep more than sex. This may continue for eighteen or more months. Sexual activities during this time tend toward the quiet because "we don't want to wake the baby."

Spontaneity might return when the parents begin to learn they must move quickly before baby wakes. Romance, on the other hand, may take a little longer to come back. I knew a couple who told me about their small apartment where the baby slept in their bedroom. They hung a sheet across the room so the baby couldn't see them, but they still had to be quiet.

The situation improves as the child or children reach the age—possibly six to ten years-- where they are able to occupy themselves. Adolescence is a new challenge. Children become curious and wonder what Mom and Dad are doing in their bedroom. They might sneak in to search for any signs of sexual activity such as lubricants or toys.

Busy Parents

Another challenge to a fulfilling sex life is employment. It is not unusual for one or both partners to have a career that requires long hours and/or travel. This is clearly an interruption to a satisfying sex life. People are often reduced to planning for sex.

The lifestyle of an active and growing family is busy but the world of soccer moms, Little League dads, and college parents can be rewarding and enjoyable. Sometimes, though, parents are so involved in the family as a whole that their sexual relationship suffers. They are too tired, too busy, too preoccupied to address their sex issues. It can be an unfortunate reality that after twenty years of being busy, the parents find they hardly know each other, and their sexual relationship has been moved to the back burner.

Revitalization

If the couple's sex life has suffered from neglect and preoccupation, sexual interest and a sense of romance may have been lost. Sometimes at this stage one or both may reveal that there has been infidelity at some point during the "busy" years.

A twenty-year marriage is an investment of time, energy, and companionship worth trying to preserve. Understanding and forgiveness are important to the healing process, as is an agreement to resist bringing up the disappointments during the rest of the marriage. At this point therapy should be considered and an attempt should be made to move forward and put romance and lovemaking back into the equation. It takes real work, once physical and emotional intimacy have ebbed away, to avoid divorce and to reenergize the marriage. Couples are encouraged to remember why they married each other, and to remember all the good there has been in the relationship.

Empty Nest

When the nest is finally empty and the "togetherness" is back in the relationship, a couple can have some of the most satisfying years of their marriage. Their sex life can be better than ever, but they should enjoy it while they can, because soon enough grandchildren and menopause will enter the picture. Unless grandchildren live near enough to be present much of the time, they will not likely present any challenges to a sex life. Menopause, however, does become a factor with which women and men both must contend. Yes – men also have some symptoms with menopause.

The hot flashes in women often lead to sleeping in separate beds or even separate rooms, which can interrupt a healthy and regular sex life, but if arrangements and accommodations are made, one can be managed.

During these challenging times, the sexual needs of the male and the female will vary because of aging and health concerns. The dry vagina and less rigid erections frustrate activity. Recently men have benefited from using Viagra and other medications to address erectile dysfunction. There are fewer medical solutions for women but many rely on new and improved lubricants.

Sex and Health

As people move on in life, new health concerns arise which require medications to manage them. Many of these medications have sexual side effects. Antidepressants can dull sex drive, as can blood pressure medications. Diabetes can negatively affect sexual performance in men and women. It requires creativity, patience, and love to overcome these obstacles and have some version of a pleasurable sexual relationship.

As people age there may be less intercourse and more "togetherness:" hugging, touching, and massage. Sometimes one member of a couple is less patient or willing to work with their mate on these issues and the relationship can suffer. It makes sense that a couple who has been together for years, raised a family and matured together, work out necessary supportive adjustments.

Sex and Singles

The single person faces sexual issues, too. Some single people appear to have little need for or interest in sex. But many do have sexual needs and cope with them in some fashion, whether it be non-marital sex, masturbation, or use of toys or pornography. The divorced and widowed face sexual adjustments, too. Some are relieved to have sex out of their lives, while others remain interested. Some may be interested but physically unable to perform. As men age, the medications for erectile dysfunction may become increasingly ineffective. Older women may question their desirability and be uncertain about their bodies' working properly.

When concerns or fears become too much to deal with alone, a sex therapist may be able to help.

Chapter 5
Children for a Lifetime

The Dream

What a wonderful dream it would be to have children who meet every expectation you have for them. The perfect children in a perfect marriage. The dream continues: they walk, talk, and potty train earlier than most. They are physically beautiful and healthy. They are socially appropriate at all times. They develop their talents: music, math, art, athletics. They never break any rules, never reject what their parents say, and are always obedient. They never wreck a car, they attend and graduate from college in four years, get a good job, marry a wonderful person, and have perfect children too. You may say "You must be dreaming!" and you would be right, yet most people begin their dream of parenthood by anticipating at least some of the above.

The Newborn

Soon after the first child is born parents realize that their child is an individual personality. Having a baby is certainly a dream for many, but the dream gives way to reality once the child is born. As soon as they hold their newborn they are probably asking, "Now what do we do?"

Couples can take classes to help them learn how to care for a baby, and a pediatrician can be a valuable resource. But even with help, some people struggle with managing the child, their marriage, their careers, and their own identities.

The lightning bolt of reality tells the new parents that the addition of this child to the marriage demands a series of serious adjustments.

No Sleep

Let's consider the probability of interruption of sleep for the parents. This can continue for eighteen months or more. That is a long time to go with insufficient sleep when one or both parents face going to work every day. The employer expects excellent performance, new baby or not. If one parent is at home, he or she must be able to manage the baby and the home, not to mention the marriage and self. It is a challenge to go through day after day on less sleep than one needs to function well. It also takes discipline and determination to face returning home each day to a weary spouse and a baby who may or may not have had a good day.

There are times when both parents wonder when they will have time, energy, and mood sufficient to relate to each other as a married couple. These demands can seriously interrupt the marriage for a period of time. Too often the parents put their relationship after the needs of the child as marriage gives way to family. It is not inevitable, however, that the marriage suffer, but it takes effort to maintain the relationship through these difficult times. Parents must resist the guilt that they may feel when they take care of themselves apart from the child. They should realize that a significant gift they can give their child is parents who are happily married to each other.

It is not easy to maintain the marriage within the family structure. The children may resent being left out occasionally and they may try to make the parents feel guilty. Parents must remember that everyone suffers when the marriage is not healthy.

Step Children

Another stress on marriage and the family which has become more common in the past few decades is the scenario of "his children, her children, their children." This is a by-product of the growing rate of divorce. The stress factors are limited time, energy and finances; resentment over how one spouse treats the children of the other; perceived loyalties of a parent to kids or spouse; and jealousy between and among the children. There can be grandparents, aunts, and uncles on all sides making demands. Some grandparents have gone to court to have visitation rights to children now in a second marriage situation. This web of relationships requires understanding, compromise, tolerance and a loving attitude by all in order for a marriage to remain healthy. Often this kind of situation requires family counseling for positive results.

Children We Like

"Oh, that was just like his grandfather, isn't that cute."

It is natural to see similarities between our children and people to whom they are related. Sometimes it is cute, but not always. The behaviors we like, we encourage; the ones we don't we work to eliminate. We may see some of the behaviors in ourselves. It is an unfortunate reality that, although we are taught to love the child and dislike the behavior, instead we love a child who behaves the way we want them to, while shunning and rejecting a child who behaves the way we don't. In our efforts to eliminate characteristics we dislike, we often become critical, which can contribute to low self esteem and create a self-critical attitude in the child.

"Like father, like son."
"The apple doesn't fall far from the tree."

Most of us have heard or said these things from time to time. Being loving and approving usually generates the same response from our children. It is also true of less rewarding behavior. For example, parents who are substance addicts often find that the addictive behaviors are perpetuated by their children. Those behaviors usually play a significant role in mate selection. The majority of children who were raised in loving and approving families are attracted to those kind of people, while the children of addicts who criticized or abused them often choose mates with similar habits.

In order to break the cycle, people must recognize the characteristics with which they were raised and use strict self-discipline to resist attraction to people who are not good for them. Unfortunately, those accustomed to the addictive, critical, or abusive lifestyle often feel "comfortable" in it because it is familiar to them.

The first three years of a child's life is when she learns love and anger and ways to express them. The years from three to twelve are self-image development years. Adolescence carries self-image into adulthood.

Behavior traits have their start early in life. If parents and their marriage survive the swimming lessons, soccer games, school plays, and summer camp, they then need to prepare to say "goodbye" to their children who are moving on to pursue college, the armed services, or the world of work. The transition to an empty nest can be difficult. It is a healthy marriage which enables parents to cope.

Chapter 6
His and Her Midlife Transitions

As you were breaking up yet another fight or wiping fingerprints off the windows, did you ever think, "Will they ever grow up?" The schedule with children at home keeps parents very busy. Family activities can be fun and fulfilling, but the breakneck, often constant pace can wear down even the most dedicated parent.

And at the snap of a finger, time has passed and children are out on their own – and there you sit. Most parents feel a sense of relief at first. They almost think they have gone deaf, it is so quiet. Then, after recuperating, they actually begin to miss all the noise and action and wonder how they will fill their time and go on from here.

Now the real togetherness kicks in. You may decide that those busy twenty years have kept us so occupied that now we are strangers. You look at each other and wonder who this person is. Yes, you were somewhat aware of changes taking place over the years, but you were too busy and too tired to talk about them.

The empty nest is a great opportunity to catch your breath and get reacquainted, assess the marriage, and work on a plan for the future. This is a good time to remember Life Priorities in Chapter 2.

The Affair

Divorce is not unusual after the nest is empty. Couples often feel they've grown apart over the years. Possibly there were marital problems along the way, but the couple stayed together for the children's sake. Unfortunately, they can do the children a disservice in this way.

I do not advocate divorce, but children feel the tension and stress in their parents' marriage and suffer because of it. Divorce may be easier on the children than twenty years of anger and hostility. At least a divorce is eventually over and all can go on with their lives.

The busy years can also be complicated when one or both spouses has an affair. Empty nest has been known to be the time when infidelity is confessed.

Work at It

Most marriages survive the empty nest and most even survive infidelity, but it takes immense effort on both spouse's parts to be forgiving. Marital counseling can be a great help. Also, if a couple can get through the trauma of an affair and stay together, it is advisable to resist bringing it up in every disagreement and hammering one's partner for the next twenty years. Bitterness is certainly no way to finish a life together.

The Job

About the time empty nest occurs there often comes a change in career situation which warrants a move. The move can be drudgery or it can be an adventure, depending on the attitude people choose to take.

Finances

College costs are through the roof these days. A move because of change in employment usually involves buying a new house. A possible second home, financial help for married children and, later, grandchildren, all stress family finances. If you are forty years old and you still do not have a retirement plan, you are running late. Family financial planning is much more complicated than many people can manage on their own. This is why more and more of us are seeking help from a Certified Financial Planner (C.F.P.).

Some immediately think of a large and expensive investment company, but a local planner knows your community, can be more personal in developing a plan for your individual needs, and usually costs less.

Menopause

Another dilemma known to the Empty Nest Group is menopause. There are plenty of jokes and "humorous" remarks that can be made about it, but it is often difficult for the woman who endures the hot flashes, chills, irritability, and decisions about hormone replacement, about which there is no overwhelming medical consensus. Menopause is a physical strain for the wife and an emotional strain for both spouses, even when the issue is only whether the house is too hot or too cool. A friend whose wife was menopausal once told me that his house was so cold that "you could hang meat in it."

It can take up to twenty years to get through this phase of life. It is important to stay cool.

In-Laws

"Who are these people?!"

A new son- or daughter-in-law with attached relatives can be an exciting and enjoyable addition to a family or an arduous and dreadful experience. The adjustment to having a new family member can be complicated by the feeling that the person who married your child is not good enough. The other family may feel the same way about your child.

It is wise for both families to become better acquainted and to work at resolving negative attitudes about each other and the children involved.

When grandchildren come along, occasionally one set of grandparents takes control and dominates enough to make it difficult for the other set to have a positive and regular relationship with the grandchildren. I have heard of some grandparents who required an appointment for the other grandparents to visit or take the children, even to the extent of making it an annual one. Some grandparents have gone to court to obtain visitation rights. These machinations seem unnecessary if there is no evidence of neglect, abuse, or drug use on either side, and a warfare situation may prove detrimental to the children and their family relationships. It is in everyone's best interest to be mature people and take the view that it is best for the kids to have a reasonable, intact family. This includes both sides.

Divorce or Death of a Spouse

I recently overheard a conversation which was a heated argument over the question of whether a divorce or death of a spouse was the worst. The widow in the group was convinced that no one knew how difficult it was for her to watch her husband suffer through his illness and finally die. The divorced woman argued that her divorce, in its willfulness, was more difficult and painful. The widow claimed that her grief was worse because death is final; she would never see her husband again. The divorcee countered that seeing and hearing about her ex-husband was harder because she was constantly reminded of their married life and the intact family that had been lost; her grief was perpetual.

Each case has its own grief and suffering can come in unique ways. Certainly the loss of a spouse under any circumstances is traumatic. A death is final and leaves an emptiness which may never be filled again. Often memory makes the lost spouse into a saint, letting negatives drop away. Divorce, on the other hand, involves the loss of a once-loving relationship and family ties, which can be re-lived each time one hears things about or sees the ex-spouse. I know a number of divorced people who check the obituaries to see if their exes are still alive. Some probably hope to see the announcement. Most, though, just care enough to want to know.

Grief is clearly present in both situations. The subject of grief is important enough to have its own chapter. There is loneliness, sorrow, anger, and regret associated with the loss of a spouse under any circumstances.

Dating Again

A widowed friend once expressed exasperation about people who kept trying to connect her with available men. She was usually embarrassed and uncomfortable during the contrived meetings.

Dating after divorce or widowhood can be frightening and unsettling. It is also a lot of work and, at times, inconvenient. A woman in her seventies told me she was tired of dating old men who just wanted to have sex. She said she was sorry that medications to relieve erectile dysfunction had ever been invented.

Usually when people date later in life they bring some amount of "baggage" with them. One elderly widow, when asked if she was interested in pursuing another relationship with a man, responded: "It will take me years to clear out all the junk my husband accumulated over the years. Another old man will bring even more junk. I think I'll pass."

His children, her children, his money, her money, his will, hers, her health problems, his – the list goes on. Baggage is to be expected in late-in-life marriages.

Recognizing the stress points in your midlife transitions is vital. Discussing them and making the necessary adjustments are crucial to happiness and a marriage's survival. If heartfelt communication can't resolve the issues, counseling is the best option.

Chapter 7
Aging Parents

When we become aware of the reality of our parents' aging, it can be an emotional jolt. We are the children; they are the parents – but now the roles seem to be reversing. Some children never make the switch, but most of us gradually take on the parenting of our parents. Often this transition is met with reluctance by all parties.

Care to the End

A childhood friend recently called me to talk about the fact that she had been diagnosed with Alzheimer's Disease. She was clearly shaken. She went on to say that it had been her daughter who had brought the changes in her behavior to her and her family's attention. Certainly it was hard for the daughter to observe the changes and address them. It was just as difficult for my friend and her husband to accept the reality of the diagnosis. Children and other relatives are prone to thinking that they will take care of their parents to the end, convinced they will keep them at home and will "never put them in a nursing home."

Never say never.

The Decision

As a psychological consultant to nursing homes, I often met with families who were struggling with the question of what was best for their elderly loved one. I commended them for wanting to care for their parent at home, but when the effort was becoming overwhelming and when it was no longer beneficial for the parent, it was time, I counseled, to consider alternatives. Frequently the aging patient suffers more pain and discomfort when they are receiving what is really not the appropriate treatment at home. At that time it is more humane and a relief to both patient and caregivers to place the parent in a situation where there is twenty-four-hour care. The children are not always aware that they may be hurting their parent more by keeping him or her at home.

It can be agonizing when the reality hits that it is time to consider assisted living or a nursing home. There is inevitably at least some guilt. But the realization that the parent will be better cared for elsewhere or by others eventually dawns, and the search for the appropriate environment begins.

Evaluate

It is not easy to judge the merits of an eldercare facility. Adult children new to the process can be overwhelmed by emotion, much less have any idea what they should be looking for. It is helpful to know that there are certain criteria that should be met which can be used to narrow down the choices and make the final decision easier. An interview with the director of admissions at any facility will clarify these considerations.

1) The Room

Rooms and apartments at various locations throughout the facility should be viewed. It is important to see occupied spaces to evaluate how much and what kind of furniture is appropriate, accessibility of the bathroom, sun exposure, and, of course, cost.

2) The Food

The food service should be evaluated for these points: where, when, and by whom it is prepared; whether a dietician is supervising patients' menus; and the setting in which food is eaten. Patients might take some meals in their rooms and others in the dining room. If meals are in a dining room, it is relevant to know how the patient will arrive there and with whom he will eat. There should be staff observing how well the patient is eating – did she eat her meal? Or just her dessert? And it is crucial to know that if the time were to come when feeding was necessary, that this would be addressed.

3) Health Care

Families should determine how medications are obtained, paid for, and administered to the patient, including supervision that assures that the patient is indeed taking the medication. A nurse or other medical personnel should be present if a doctor is not always there, and it is important to know what emergency procedures are in place.

If a parent lives long enough, he or she will eventually require more health care than an assisted living facility can offer. Some assisted living homes have skilled nursing facilities attached to their campuses or agencies. It should be determined what the procedures and criteria are for transfer from one environment to another, and what the change in cost will be.

4) Hygiene and Security

Bathing, dental care, grooming, and other hygiene needs should be discussed with caregivers. It is also important to know the security measures taken to protect the patients and their possessions.

5) Legal Concerns

Wills should be determined to be current while the loved one is still competent, and estate planning should be completed. There should be copies of living wills and final directives in the hands of attending physicians and other relevant agencies as well as safely in the keeping of adult children. I have seen patients and families suffer when there have been no directives in place and no durable power of attorney appointed. The holder of health care power of attorney should ideally be geographically as close to the patient as possible.

6) Hospice

The medical professionals involved in a patient's care are obligated to do all they can to keep a patient alive, even with directives. When the end is near, much grief can be avoided by placing a patient in a hospice program where he or she can finish life in peace and comfort. This is usually a relief to all involved, including medical people who appreciate the futility of heroic measures in some circumstances.

7) Long Term Insurance

Long term health care insurance is worth considering in some situations. The younger the patient, the lower the premiums. Between sixty and sixty-five is a reasonable age to begin planning. For planning purposes I refer to the American Association of Homes and Services for the Aging (AAHSA) study of 2006 which cites the following:

Length of stay for men vs. women in nursing homes:

1 year – men 79%; women 74%
3-5 years – men 13%; women 13%
5 years – men 4%; women 7%

It is worthy to note that 79% of men live one year or less after admission. The study does not include the second year. I have observed that in the nursing homes I have visited the female population is usually larger than the male population.

Therefore it is not usually necessary for men to buy more than two years of coverage. Women tend to live longer and do end up in nursing facilities more frequently and for longer periods. This is a consideration when considering long term care coverage. There are insurance professionals who can advise families on the appropriate coverage for their situations.

Taking care of aging parents can be an emotionally trying experience. Parents can be resentful and cruel to their caregivers, including their children, because they are resisting giving up the control they have heretofore possessed. They can become paranoid about their money, house, and material belongings. They might feel that everyone is stealing from them and waiting for them to die so they can have their stuff. Their children frequently feel guilty and hurt, but it is helpful to know, in the end, that everything was done for the good of the parents regardless of whether they recognized or appreciated it.

Chapter 8
How Time Flies

"My, how time flies" is a statement often made in dejected tones at birthday, retirement, and New Year's parties. Eventually many of us start wondering "where the time went."

At the time I am writing this I am aware that both my children are in their forties. It seems only a few years ago that they were playing with dolls and in tree forts, struggling to be cooperative with each other. It is a wrench to accept that both my parents are deceased. In my mind, I can hear my mother playing the piano and my father and their friends singing along.

In reality, though, I am getting older. The passage of time sometimes feels as if it is at lighting speed. I can't believe I've arrived here so soon.

At this point in one's life, it is time to start getting down to the business of aging and consider these questions:

1) How will I know it is time to retire?

2) How does one retire?

3) What should I do after retirement?

4) Do I have enough money or income?

5) What is the state of my/our health insurance?

6) Should I/we move?

7) How am I coping with aging, attendant health concerns, and the approaching inevitability of death? Am I suffering from melancholia, grief, depression, or denial about any of these?

8) Is/was my life meaningful?

9) Will my religious faith or spiritual grounding give me confidence when facing my own death?

The indicators for retirement vary among individuals. Some people are forced to retire because of regulations at their place of employment. You might work 30 years, then told to retire. There might be a mandatory age of retirement. Some are forced to retire as a surprise at fifty-five. Involuntary retirement can be a shock – it was not predicted and there was no time to prepare. To be suddenly out of a job after many years indeed strikes at one's need for control and can damage one's confidence and self-image. The feeling of helplessness can lead to despair and depression.

A gentleman once came to me for counseling because he had been laid off from a job he had held for many years. In his early fifties he was unemployed, depressed, and without a plan. He came to me for several sessions for help dealing with the trauma, and I also administered several occupational tests to identify his aptitudes and areas of interest. His career had been spent in middle management in a corporation. His test results strongly recommended that he either teach English or study Library Science. These were new ideas to him. After some time and discussion he decided to pursue Library Science. He has been a happy librarian ever since.

The value of emotional and career counseling cannot be overstated in circumstances such as these.

People who have been self-employed can face similar challenges, whether their careers have been in some sort of private practice or in the business field. It is unsettling to voluntarily walk away from a lucrative and enjoyable work life into retirement. Often individuals in this category reduce their hours and slowly cut back, eventually giving up work altogether. Sometimes this happens after people have become increasingly aware that they are losing competence, and do not want to be in the position of causing harm. It can take varying lengths of time to accept the need to retire, to be introspective enough to see that one is no longer as efficient or as capable as heretofore. Occasionally people can't give up and work long after they have lost their edge in their field.

Do I have enough money?

This is a question one should be asking at least ten years before expected retirement age. It is usually too late to make a significant difference in one's financial future a year or two from retirement. Often people depend on the company pension, if there is one, and have little or no savings or investments.

In Chapter 2 I mentioned one of my consulting contracts which was to counsel local factory workers who were within one year of retirement. We covered many topics, from adjusting to being newly retired and at home full-time, to learning to spend more time with a spouse or alone. It was alarming that most of the retirees had little or no savings after thirty or more years of earning excellent wages. They had spent all they had made. The one advantage for most of them was that their homes were paid for. Other than that, most only had social security and a pension on which to live. Most of them came to realize the necessity of a savings plan, but one year before retirement is too late to do much in the way of financial planning.

The historic typical company pension is falling away. Social Security is not as predictable as it once was. A 401K, an IRA, investments, and a financial planner are good tools for mapping out a financially comfortable retirement.

Health insurance can be a serious financial drain after retirement. Fewer corporations are now offering affordable coverage for the duration of post-retirement life. Medicare and supplemental insurance are better than nothing, but there is a litany of expenses not covered by these, and the cost is higher every year. At this writing, my experience indicates that it is reasonable to plan on $5000 - $10,000 per year in costs not covered by insurance.

The question about whether or not to move is common after retirement. A larger percentage of people stay where they are, but many decide to move to a warmer climate or to be nearer to family. It is a major adjustment to move to a new state, climate, and culture after being in the same place for a long time. Some people try several potential areas each for a short period of time to evaluate their comfort there. Others follow their neighbors and friends. I knew a group of people in the upper Midwest who all had lived on the same street for years and who knew each other well. They all retired at about the same time and together moved to a city in Florida to be neighbors there, too. Whether or not, and when, to move is a decision that requires soul-searching and a lot of research.

Some people say, " I wonder how I had time to work, I'm so busy since I retired." They fill their days with more of their old favorite activities like golf, bridge, eating out, and reading. Sometimes they find new hobbies, volunteer work, or even part-time jobs to fill the time and fend off boredom. If health allows it, it is important to not just sit at home and wonder how to fill the days.

Retirement lasts longer today than it did twenty years ago. Medical opinions indicate that seventy-year-old people have health equal to that of most fifty-year-olds of two decades ago. Our parents and especially our grandparents were quite old at seventy. Today the average seventy-year-old is active and alert and has a much longer life expectancy.

A difficult but practical and necessary feature of aging is coping with end-of-life decisions. During illness, a final directive is important in order to tell all involved whether one wants heroic measures to be used to maintain life under any circumstances, or whether palliative or intermediate care is all that is desired when death is impending. The appropriate papers are available at most hospitals at no cost, and it is vital to have these filled out before such decisions are necessary. This documentation does not usually require the services of an attorney.

Funeral planning is a growing industry. Most funeral facilities have at least one employee whose job it is to explain and help plan various aspects of the process. There are many decisions to be made about what type of service is wanted, whether burial or cremation is desired, what kind of casket is appropriate and affordable, and whether one has a realistic idea of the costs involved. Funeral insurance is becoming more common. The funeral home sells a consumer a policy which covers the current cost of the planned funeral, no matter how costs increase over the ensuing years. The insurance company earns interest on the policy paid, which usually makes up the difference if the eventual funeral costs more. If the cost is lower at the time of death, the family usually receives a refund.

It is important to remember that as people age they sometimes don't remember what they have planned. I knew one elderly couple who bought nine different funeral insurance policies, forgetting that they had already done it.

After all the planning is finished, an extra step is to remember to plan a legacy – a significant contribution to family, mankind, and God.

Chapter 9
Coping With Grief

Grief is a natural and expected part of living. There are so many life events that cause and contribute to grief that they cannot be listed. A review of the topics of this booklet gives a partial list, from the loss of control, difficulty in relationships, and the hazards of raising children to the trauma of transitional periods, deteriorating health, and death of loved ones, life is a series of losses, and the response to significant loss is grief.

When one senses the fleeting essence of time, one can experience grief. The realization that we are aging perceptibly confirms that we are losing control and that we are having to form new identities.

Divorce at any age and certainly widowhood cause grief, and the practical tasks that must be accomplished after either event can prolong the grief process.

While funeral planning is practical and encouraged, it can be a sort of grief as a person contemplates his own death. Funeral home staff are used to assisting in this process – grief is not new to them.

It goes without saying that things like chronic illness, the death of a child or other family member, loss of friend-ships, fire, and flood are natural predisposing factors of grief. An analysis of grief and coping mechanisms are useful in any grief situation.

Grief takes its opportunity when the strongest human drive, control, is threatened. Grief then naturally follows a nearly standard and predictable sequence. My interpretation of that is as follows:

1) Control
2) Helplessness
3) Denial
4) Fear
5) Anger
6) Depression
7) Bargaining
8) Acceptance

This list shows the progression of grief through its stages. As the list shows, once feelings of control are lost, feelings of helplessness ensue. The helpless feeling is commonly resisted by use of denial. Denial helps for a while until the full realization of loss hits like a ton of bricks. That is when fear and anger take over. People become scared and defiant toward others and toward God for the loss being experienced. Then there is a transition into depression as the reality becomes a part of waking life. A lengthy depression takes so much energy and can be so painful that human beings naturally begin to lean toward a better way to cope. Often that is some sort of bargaining position, as if a deal can be reached with God or the universe. A search begins for an attitude or position from which one can begin to accept the reason for the grief. Even if a full recovery never takes place, eventually a stance is found from which enough comfort is derived to finally accept and find peace with the loss.

Timetable

"When will I get over this?!"

It is helpful to know that grief often follows a predictable timetable. The length of each stage is dependent on the event and the person's initial preparedness and wherewithal, but knowledge of the stages may offer some hope for getting through to other side.

1) The initial stage after a loss, a person generally feels numb. He can't quite take it in. He may not be aware of other feelings and may be nonfunctional emotionally or even physically.

2) In Stage 2, the person tends to behave mechanically. He functions to exist, but seems only to be going through the motions. As time passes, functioning progresses toward less mechanical and more fully functional.

3) In Stage 3, the person improves gradually, is able to feel emotion more, and begins to move through the world without a shroud of pain.

4) Stage 4 is more hopeful. There are certainly continued "down" periods, but "ups" are more regular.

The above four stages are indicator of sequence, but people may find that they move back and forth between the stages at times. After moving along to stage 3, people can wake up one day feeling like they are back in stage 1 or 2.

Counseling can greatly speed and assist the healing process.

Some people never resolve their grief. Others take years, depending on the predisposing event, but eventually most people find a position or attitude that helps them finally put most of their grief away and move on.

There are many coping mechanisms available that may offer short-term relief, but the relief is bought at a hefty price and may cause grief of its own. Drug and alcohol abuse, overeating or anorexia, sexual promiscuity, and unnecessary risk-taking may be tempting, but it is healthier to trust God and loved ones while turning toward making life meaningful and positive once again.

Chapter 10
There is Always Hope

The previous chapters have discussed life situations for which we have very little training or preparation. They also presented coping attitudes and actions that will help people to "deal with it." This chapter, on Hope, offers just that.

In Chapter 1, the sequence of the progression from loss of control through death was explained.

Remember, our strongest drive is for control. When situations occur that threaten our perceived control, we begin to feel helpless and start working harder to maintain the control. This effort can be a frenzy, throwing us into a state of heightened anxiety. It is detrimental to our health and our relationships. A healthier approach is to do what we can to maintain or regain control without causing us physical or mental illness. We owe it to all we love and to God to take care of ourselves. We gain little if we become ill in the struggle for control. Even Jesus stopped working miracles and separated himself from the throngs surrounding him. He left them often to be alone, eat, sleep, and pray so that he could offer his best the next day. He had a mission to accomplish and so do we all. So, we must do what we can without becoming ill. Then we must do what is contradictory to our nature: we must let go. We do what we can, stay healthy, then hand our concerns over to God.

We have very little training in recognizing when we can do nothing more and need to trust God for the solution. Trusting takes practice. Many clergy have said, "Let go and let God." They never explain how to do that. Here is how to do it (with practice):

Giving up control contradicts our nature. For example, in my youth, I played football. I was not a large, brawny man, but at 180 lbs. I could run faster than many. My position was "wide out," or the person who ran down the field to catch a pass and run for a touchdown. There were times when a defensive back or line backer stood between me and the goal. When it looked like I would be smashed by the defender, I would hand the ball to someone else. I wasn't injured as often and was able to play another day. It was not easy to give up the ball and the possible glory of a touchdown, but when I felt helpless I was willing to let go and leave it to someone else. This is where our faith comes into plan. It is easier to be a believer than to trust God; belief is our first step. The transition from belief to trust is a giant leap, placing us in a position to put our faith into practice, to let go and actually let God take over.

A better understanding of the core message of Christianity will help in our quest to learn how to trust God.

In the Old Testament, the contract, or covenant, between God and humans involved the idea that God looked directly down at us and at our sinful state. God provided a system of sacrificial rites for us to follow in order to have his forgiveness. But the ceremonies had to be repeated each time His followers requested forgiveness.

It was clear that the sacrificial system was only a temporary way for people to obtain God's forgiveness. The hope clearly was that the Messiah would come and permanently cover our sinfulness once and for all. This is what happened in the New Testament – a new covenant. It gave us the Son of God, the Christ who paid the price for the sinfulness of the world with his death. His was the final sacrifice to end all sacrifices.

Therefore, under the new covenant, the blood of Christ covers our sinfulness when each of us becomes God's child by accepting Christ as the divine mediator between God and humankind. Under the new contract, God no longer looks directly down at us and our sinfulness. He looks through the blood of Christ and does not see the sin. He sees only us. Isaiah 1:18 says, "Though your sins be as scarlet they shall be as white as snow."

This is the knowledge human beings need in order to make the transition between believing and trusting. The information is only half the procedure. Accepting the message and literally leaning on and trusting God is the other half.

Exercise

The following applies to anyone, regardless of religious identification.

Practice trusting by faith, knowing that within a few minutes you will be anxious again. When you are aware of anxiety returning, you know that you are still trying to control and are not trusting. Try again, and again. Each time you attempt trust, you will trust a little longer. It is like weight lifting. You become stronger as you keep lifting.

Recently my good friend learned that he had an incurable illness and that death would be coming soon. He had studied most of the well-known religions of the world. When I asked him what he was thinking to help him face death, he said he was not able to fully understand any of the religions he had studied, including Christianity. But he remembered that Jesus had said, "Trust me." And so he did. He made the transition from believer to truster and died peacefully.

When dealing with life, we do what we can to maintain control without becoming ill. Then we practice making the transition from belief to trust. In trust we regain control and hope.

May God bless you in your journey.

Breinigsville, PA USA
12 November 2009
227398BV00002B/40/P

9 781438 950662